"Hope is patience with the lamp lit."
Tertullian

Illustration © James Newman Grey from *Colour in Hope: Postcards*, published in 2018 by Lion Hudson IP Limited

"*Hope*
Smiles from the threshold of the
year to come
Whispering 'It will be happier…'"
Alfred Tennyson

Illustration © James Newman Grey from *Colour in Hope: Postcards*, published in 2018 by Lion Hudson IP Limited

> *"We must accept finite disappointment, but we must never lose infinite hope."*
> Martin Luther King Jr.

"Be joyful in hope, patient in affliction, faithful in prayer."
Romans 12:12

Illustration © James Newman Grey from *Colour in Hope: Postcards*, published in 2018 by Lion Hudson IP Limited

"Hope is the pillar that holds up the world. Hope is the dream of a waking man."
Pliny the Elder

*"Hope is like the sun,
which, as we journey toward it,
casts the shadow of our burden
behind us."*
Samuel Smiles

*"Hope is patience with the
lamp lit."*
Tertullian

Illustration © James Newman Grey from *Colour in Hope:
Postcards*, published in 2018 by Lion Hudson IP Limited

"Hope
Smiles from the threshold of the
year to come
Whispering 'It will be happier…'"
Alfred Tennyson

"*We must accept finite disappointment, but we must never lose infinite hope.*"
Martin Luther King Jr.

"Be joyful in hope, patient in affliction, faithful in prayer."
Romans 12:12

"Hope is the pillar that holds up the world. Hope is the dream of a waking man."
Pliny the Elder

"Hope is like the sun,
which, as we journey toward it,
casts the shadow of our burden
behind us."
Samuel Smiles

Illustration © James Newman Grey from *Colour in Hope:*
Postcards, published in 2018 by Lion Hudson IP Limited

"Hope is patience with the lamp lit."
Tertullian

"Hope
Smiles from the threshold of the
year to come
Whispering 'It will be happier...'"
Alfred Tennyson

Illustration © James Newman Grey from *Colour in Hope: Postcards*, published in 2018 by Lion Hudson IP Limited

"*We must accept finite disappointment, but we must never lose infinite hope.*"
Martin Luther King Jr.

"Be joyful in hope, patient in affliction, faithful in prayer."
Romans 12:12

*"Hope is the pillar that holds up
the world. Hope is the dream of a
waking man."*
Pliny the Elder

Illustration © James Newman Grey from *Colour in Hope:
Postcards*, published in 2018 by Lion Hudson IP Limited

"Hope is like the sun,
which, as we journey toward it,
casts the shadow of our burden
behind us."
Samuel Smiles

Illustration © James Newman Grey from *Colour in Hope:*
Postcards, published in 2018 by Lion Hudson IP Limited

"Hope is patience with the lamp lit."
Tertullian

Illustration © James Newman Grey from *Colour in Hope: Postcards*, published in 2018 by Lion Hudson IP Limited

"Hope
Smiles from the threshold of the
year to come
Whispering 'It will be happier…'"
Alfred Tennyson